Help Me Be Good
Teasing

Joy Berry
Illustrated by Bartholomew

Joy Berry Books
New York

This book is about T.J. and his sister, Tami.

Reading about T.J. and Tami can help you understand and deal with teasing.

People are teasing you when they annoy you or make fun of you in playful ways.

Has anyone ever teased you about
the way you look?

Has anyone ever teased you about the way you think and feel?

Has anyone ever teased you about what you say or do?

Has anyone ever teased you about what you like and do not like?

When someone teases you, you might feel frustrated and embarrassed.

You might get upset and become angry.

People who tease often enjoy frustrating and embarrassing others.

They enjoy upsetting others.

Thus, you encourage them to continue teasing you when you become frustrated, embarrassed, or upset.

Do not become frustrated, embarrassed, or upset if you want someone who is teasing you to stop.

Do these things instead:
- Ignore anyone who teases you.
- Walk away from the person if you cannot ignore him or her.
- Do not stay around anyone who continues to tease you.

It is important to treat others the way you want to be treated.

If you do not like being teased, you should not tease others.

Try not to tease.

Do not discuss another person's private thoughts or feelings unless you have the person's permission to do so.

Try not to tease.

Do not say embarrassing things about anyone
in front of others.

Try not to tease.

Avoid saying things that might hurt someone else's feelings.

This is a good rule to follow:
  If you cannot say something nice about someone,
  avoid saying anything at all.

If you follow this rule, you will avoid hurting
other people's feelings.

It is important to treat other people the way you want to be treated.

If you do not want to be teased, you should not tease others.

Cover Design & Art Direction: John Bellaud
Cover Illustration & Art Production: Geoff Glisson

Production Location: HX Printing, Guangzhou, China
Date of Production: July 2010
Cohort: Batch 1
9036
Printed in China
ISBN 978-1-60577-141-0